Eco-Autonomo

Organizations

Decentralized, Distributed and Autonomous Organizations; An Operational Viewpoint of Complex Adaptive Systems

Natty Gur

Contributors: John Tyce, Brian Matthews

Reviewer: Anna Romain

Editor: Laura L. Mariani

Galaxies CAS LLC

Table of Contents

Why Does Our Management System Need To Change?

Humankind has witnessed many positive changes over the last 100 years. People are living longer, essential utilities are standard in most homes, literacy has increased from 20 percent to 88 percent, and technology has made communication around the world faster and easier. In addition, minority populations are gaining more traction in the quest for equal rights (albeit not as quickly as they may like) and communities are experiencing fewer instances of violence and war than ever before ("The Better Angels of Our Nature: Why Violence Has Declined" by Steven Pinker). There is one element of modern life, however, that hasn't changed much: the way that we manage, organize and motivate people in the workplace.

The concept of management as we know it today was introduced in 1911 by American inventor and mechanical engineer Frederick Winslow Taylor in his book, "The Principles of Scientific Management." In summary, Taylor's concept separated employees into two categories—thinkers and workers—within the workplace. In the factory environments that were common at the time, thinkers used scientific methods to manage workers on production lines.

Taylor's concept of scientific management is based on four main principles: 1) Assigning work based on scientific study of the tasks to be carried out, 2) Selecting and training individuals to perform specific tasks, 3) Providing individuals with clear instructions so they know exactly what to do and then supervising them while they do it, and 4) Separating managers' and workers' job functions so that managers are able to "scientifically" plan what needs to be done and workers can perform the actions assigned. While these principles have changed somewhat since Taylor's time, the basic idea of separating thinkers from workers has remained the same.

Complicated Versus Complex Worlds

Taylor's notion of scientific management began as a noble idea that ultimately contributed to the success of the second industrial revolution. In today's world, however, this system has become a problematic structure with the potential to negatively impact the success and survival of modern businesses.

Why has "Taylorism" become such a problem? The reason can be explained scientifically in two words: "complicated" and "complex." In science, these words refer to types of systems and the difference between their elements is defined as follows:

- The behavior and reactions of **complicated elements** in a system are predictable. A smartphone, for example, is a complicated element: Tap its screen and it behaves predictably.

- The behavior and reactions of **complex elements** in a system are unexpected. People are complex elements:

If you ask a group of people a question, their
responses are unpredictable.

Using these definitions, it's easy to comprehend that the
economic market was "complicated" a century ago. Back
then, the market had hard geographical boundaries, few
industry competitors and even fewer surprises, making it
feasible to foresee what might happen within an industry. That
consistency made it possible for business owners to focus
their attention on what was happening inside their factories
and devise ways to optimize production. Taylor's
management system was created to help simplify this
complicated world and his method was a huge success due
to the world's predictability.

In contrast, the current economic market is "complex": It is
global, has no geographic boundaries, and is packed with
worldwide competitors that have the potential to create new
and unexpected realities for other businesses within their
sphere. In other words, the pace of innovation has increased,
and companies can no longer complacently and exclusively
focus on the technologies that led to the success they have
today. Through innovation, giants can be toppled by smaller
players (Think Kodak, Nokia, and Research in Motion).

As a result, humans are now living in a volatile, uncertain,
complex and ambiguous (VUCA) world. The processes that
were created for the previous, complicated world no longer fit
the current environment. To thrive, humans must devise
different methods for dealing with the complexities of a VUCA
world.

Surviving in a Complex World

In the years following the second industrial revolution, complexities in the economic market grew exponentially with the introduction of new occupations based on data manipulation and collaboration (which created new business values), virtual commodities (from data to currency), the development of virtual infrastructures to support such commodities, and the expansion of labor resources to include robotics and artificial intelligence. With the addition of new, Internet-educated generations into the workforce (generations that recognize the value that organizations based on decentralized, distributed and autonomous principles can provide), complexity is poised to gain further momentum.

As mentioned earlier, in the complicated world that inspired Taylorism, factory employees were divided into two groups: workers and thinkers. In today's complex world, however, that division no longer exists. Now, workers (that is, anyone interacting within or around a company's environment including its customers, stockholders, and suppliers; and even city and state officials, etc.) must be "thinkers" as well, often working in silos created by their areas of specialization, further constraining the company's ability to be successful.

Suffice it to say, companies trying to run twenty-first-century businesses using twentieth-century workplace practices are cracking under the pressure (2012 Global Workforce Study, Towers Watson, July 2012)[i]. For evidence that management systems based on Taylor's century-old theory are failing, look no further than the Internet for articles highlighting the decline of employee engagement ("Employee Engagement is Declining Worldwide," Forbes, June 1, 2017)[ii], the rise of the freelance workforce ("Are We Ready For A Workforce That Is 50% Freelance?," Forbes, October 17, 2017)[iii], the number of companies disappearing from the Fortune 500 list (Fortune 500 Firms 1955 v. 2017: Only 60 Remain, Thanks to the Creative Destruction that Fuels Economic Prosperity," American Enterprise Institute, October 17, 2017)[iv], and the negative exponential growth in the lifespan of companies ("Why Half of the S&P 500 Companies Will Be Replaced in the Next Decade," Inc., March 23, 2016)[v]. For further insights, author Richard Ronald Nason's book, "It's Not Complicated: The Art and Science of Complexity for Business Success"[vi] details the impacts of conducting business in a complex world as well.

To live and operate in a complex world, it's only logical that humans use complex systems (such as the human brain, the economic market, and even the universe) principles to run business and organization that need to operate in a complex world. To survive and thrive into the next century and beyond, companies need to modify their organizational structures based on these concepts. Only then will businesses be able to do the things they need to do—motivate people, increase performance, and spark innovation—to withstand the demands of a complex world. The ideas of a brilliant founder can build a highly successful company, but their ideas alone cannot sustain it. To stand the test of time in a VUCA marketplace, a company must leverage all of its intellectual capital. Decades of research show that the level of employee engagement and proactivity required to support this level of innovation is achieved through employee autonomy[vii].

Principles of an Eco-Autonomous Organization

Eco-Autonomous organizations are organizations that are a collection of autonomous groups that are working in decentralize way and distribute work between autonomous groups. To successfully encourage certain workplace behaviors, eco-autonomous organizations must establish explicit and easy-to-follow principles. To create an organization that is decentralized, distributed and autonomous firms should establish principles which are tangible. Unlike commonly used principles which are vague and undefined such as: accountability, balance, commitment, community, safety, diversity, empowerment, integrity, and ownership, etc. Instead, organization should establish well defined tangible principles such as those defined below.

- **Purpose**: Each group should have a clearly defined purpose that states its value (financial or social) within the organization. Every employee should know the purpose and value of his role within any group and the overall corporate entity.

- **Radical Truth**: Each member of the organization must uphold and seek the truth at all times, be true to themselves and act in accordance with the company's principles. When communicating with peers, customers, vendors and competitors, employees must always speak honestly. It's not enough for employees to *believe* that they are right—they must ensure they have the correct answer and the information or data to support it.

- **Radical Transparency**: Transparency builds trust within an organization. Employees should share information with (and never conceal anything from) their colleagues and respond transparently when providing feedback. Every member of the organization should know and understand each policy and decision from compensation to company strategy. If an employee has questions about how or why something is being done, they should ask for an explanation.

- **Learn from Mistakes**: Mistakes are part of being human; without exception, everyone makes them. To prevent errors from reoccurring, however, people have to learn from their mistakes and apply what they've learned to their work. This is the only way an organization—or an individual—can continuously improve. Eco-autonomous organizations are blame-free cultures where employees are encouraged to share their errors so that others can learn.

- **Radical Self-Awareness**: Every individual and organization has strengths and weaknesses. Being aware of these areas of excellence and vulnerability builds character, humility, and strength. Environments that actively encourage people to do and be their best foster creativity, spark innovation and increase performance. Employees should continuously strive for self-improvement, pursue opportunities to learn about themselves, and become aware of how their words and actions impact other people. Employees should be willing to share their development goals. When co-workers know what their teammates are working on, they can help each other reach their objectives.

- **Radical Self-Management**: Since the Industrial Revolution, humans have been told what to do—and how to behave—within the workplace. This practice continues in modern work environments to varying degrees. In eco-autonomous organizations, however, the goal is to hire people who can manage themselves, think proactively, identify problems, and take action to resolve them as needed.

  As individuals, the only behavior we can truly manage is our own, yet self-management cannot replace execution or accountability. On the contrary, self-management requires individuals to be responsible not only for themselves but also for their groups' performance and accountability.

  While leaders will always be needed in work environments, these roles should be awarded based on merit. Managers, on the other hand, are not required. In self-managed groups, there aren't managers to notify or complain to; each person is empowered to resolve challenges or problems as they arise.

- **Radical Multi-Functional Teams:** The siloed, single-function teams that exist within today's organizations must be broken down to create agile, multi-functional teams that will thrive in a VUCA world.

- **Fight Cognitive Bias with Data**: All humans suffer from cognitive bias (the belief that what we think is "right" and what others think is "wrong"). These subconscious beliefs often cause people to jump to conclusions and act without thinking. Thousands of years ago, making decisions instinctively saved our ancestors from predators, however, leaping to judgment today can cause serious problems in the workplace.

  Fortunately, organizations can now use data and analysis to combat these biases. By setting up functions and processes to collect as much information as possible, and using analysis to determine which processes are working and which are not, companies can use data to make decisions. However, significant decisions should never be based solely on statistics. Logic, common sense and data with sound analysis are necessary for making informed decisions.

- **Resolve Conflicts through Merit Voting**: By following the principles listed above, workers should be able to successfully engage with others. When disagreements arise, employees should use the principles above as a guide for resolving conflict. If an agreement can't be reached, the organization's merit voting system should be used to address the issue. We will discuss this concept in more detail later in this book.

Complex Adaptive Systems

Some people view their businesses as well-running machines that can be easily understood and improved. Others believe their businesses are similar to organisms or complex systems that need to be balanced routinely. This paper suggests that eco-autonomous organizations based on complex adaptive systems should be implemented to replace existing and outdated management systems in modern corporations. Before this can be done, however, organizations need to understand the attributes, behaviors, risks, advantages, and disadvantages associated with complex adaptive systems.

A complex adaptive system is a system in which many independent elements (or agents) interact, leading to emergent outcomes that are often difficult or impossible to predict simply by looking at each individual interaction. The system is adaptive because it uses a feedback loop to adapt each element—and the system as a whole—to changes as they happen. Examples of complex adaptive systems include the economy, the human brain, developing embryos, ant colonies, ecosystems, the weather, and, yes, in today's world, even corporate organizations or government entities.

Before adopting an eco-autonomous organizational model, companies must pay attention to the following attributes of a complex adaptive system:

- **Distributed Control**: With distributed control, there isn't a single, centralized control mechanism that governs system behavior. Although the interrelationships between a system's elements produce coherence, the system's overall behavior usually cannot be explained by the sum of its individual parts. To illustrate, consider that a developing embryo doesn't have any cells, nor does it have a master neuron in the brain that controls it. Similarly, if we use the economy as an example, the overall behavior observed in a fluctuating market is the result of countless decisions made by millions of individual people every day.

- **Connectivity**: Complexity results from the interrelationship, interaction and interconnectivity of the elements within a system and between a system and its environment. This implies that a decision or action by one element will influence all other related parts of a system (but not in any expected way).

- **Co-Evolution**: With co-evolution, elements in a system can change based on their interactions with one another and with the environment. Additionally, patterns of behavior can (and should) change over time.

- **Dependence on Initial Conditions**: Complex adaptive systems are sensitive due to their dependence on initial conditions, therefore, changes in the input characteristics or rules of a system do not correlate in a linear fashion with outcomes. As a result, small changes in the initial condition of a complex system can lead to unpredictable consequences even if everything in the system is causally connected in a deterministic way. This means that 1) small changes can have a surprisingly profound impact on a system's overall behavior or 2) a huge upset to the system may have no effect at all.

- **Self-Organization:** Complex adaptive systems lack a command and control hierarchy. Any coherent behavior arises from the competition, cooperation or self-organization amongst each agent. "Planning" or "managing" does not exist, rather, the system constantly adapts to find the best fit with the environment. To illustrate, imagine adding up all of the food in a town's shops and dividing it by the number of people living in the town. There would likely be a few weeks' supply of food available, yet the town has not implemented a formal control process or plan to ensure a few weeks' supply of food. A continually self-organizing system simply exists through the process of emergence and feedback.

- **Emergent Order**: The "complexity" in a complex adaptive system refers to the potential for emergent behavior in complicated and unpredictable phenomena. Each of the following examples is a system with a network comprised of many agents acting in parallel: 1) In an economy, the agents might be households; 2) In an ecosystem, the agents are species; 3) In a brain, the agents are nerve cells; and 4) In an eco-autonomous work environment, the agents are people.

Each agent within a system exists in an environment produced by its interactions with other agents in the system. There are constant actions between—and reactions to—what the other agents are doing, which means that nothing in the environment is static. These interactions produce different kinds of global properties, patterns, arrangements or configurations that cannot be predicted by understanding each particular agent. In the case of the brain, for example, consciousness is an emergent phenomenon derived from the interaction of brain cells.

- **Far from Equilibrium**: In their book, "Exploring Complexity: An Introduction," published in 1989, Gregoire Nicolis and Ilya Prigogine showed that even when a physical or chemical system is pushed away from equilibrium, it can survive and thrive. However, if a system remains at equilibrium, it will die. The "far from equilibrium" phenomenon illustrates how systems that are forced to explore their spaces of possibility will adapt and create different structures and new patterns of relationships.

- **State of Paradox**: Dynamics (interaction between system elements) in complex adaptive systems are created when both order and chaos are combined. This reinforces the idea that being on the edge of chaos is characterized by a state of paradox. Being on the edge of chaos means being in between stability and instability; competition and cooperation; and order and disorder.

- **Non-Linear**: A complex adaptive system is a non-linear, unpredictable system whose whole is greater than the sum (or average) of its parts. Therefore, even though a person may be familiar with all of the components of a system, he still may not be able to predict exactly what will happen next. Another aspect of this system's non-linearity worth noting is that cause and effect are distant in time and space.

- **Models and Feedback**: Through its agents, a complex adaptive system acquires information about its environment and its own interaction with that environment, identifies regularities in that information, condenses those regularities into a set of rules combined together into models, and acts in the real world on the basis of those models.

In every system, there are also various competing models. When the models in a system interact with the real world, they receive feedback that either influences the competition between those models or creates a brand new model. As each agent gains experience through interaction, internal models are created or modified. Once an agent gains experience, it abstracts regularities from the randomness within that experience and begins to form internal models that describe those regularities.

If an agent repeatedly exhibits a behavior that is counter-productive to its internal model, then the internal model will be modified, discarded or ignored.

On the other hand, if an agent repeatedly exhibits a behavior that is productive, then the internal model (or schema) responsible will be retained and will become dominant.

- **The Parts Can't Improve the Whole**: Remember, in a complex adaptive system, it isn't the parts that matter. Rather, it's the way those parts connect and communicate with all the other parts that create the whole. Therefore, to improve a system one must focus on the interactions between each element to understand the whole. It's important to note that focusing directly on individual components or agents can result in damage to a system.

Through history, humans were taught to understand the world by dividing systems into their constituent parts and finding ways to improve the workability of each part rather than analyzing the entire system. As a result, it's sometimes difficult for humans to grasp complex issues.

To begin building companies based on complex adaptive systems, people must be willing to abandon the methods traditionally used to understand events (such as thinking that the external environment is static) and stop conducting detailed analysis of the parts of a system. Instead, they need to take "a crude look at the whole" (as suggested by American physicist Murray Gell-Mann, 1994) and embrace a new way of thinking. Doing so will enable business leaders to create adaptable corporate entities that will thrive in the ever-changing VUCA world being shaped by new generations and technologies.

The Basic Structure of an Eco-Autonomous Organization

An eco-autonomous organization is a grouping of different functions or entities that work together in harmony to fulfill a certain objective and provide value for different elements within or outside of an organization's environment.

Eco-autonomous organizations are created and driven using a purpose- and value-based process, which does not follow the specialized (siloed) organizational structure governing most businesses today. Eco-autonomous organizations start by defining the overall purpose of the organization; then, a group of necessary functions, each with their own defined purpose, are identified to support its realization.

As shown in Figure A, below, these functions can be organized into a value chain that depicts how the organization will achieve its purpose and deliver its value. If there are several functions serving the same purpose, they may be grouped into entities within the hosting entity. Ultimately, the organizational structure of an entity can be broken down until all of the entities and functions within it reach the functional level.

Eco-autonomous organizations are not hierarchal—hierarchal relationships between entities don't exist—however, the fact that these particular elements are grouped together provides value within the system.

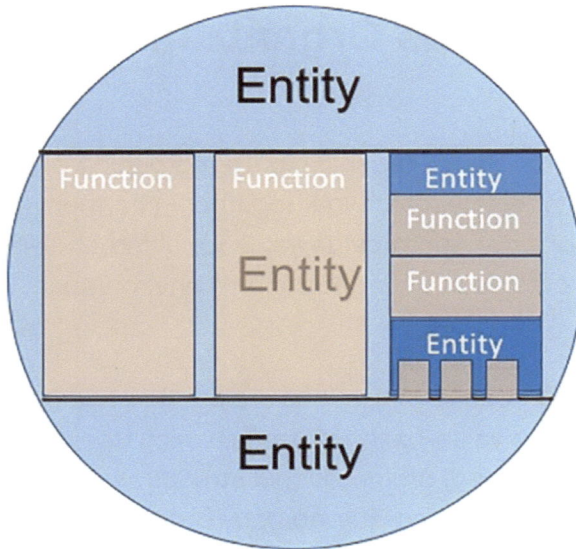

Figure A: An Eco-Autonomous Organization

The "function-based" approach used in eco-autonomous organizations arranges people based on the functions that need to be performed and not on a single area of expertise, enabling multiple skills and capabilities to be represented. This approach contradicts the common organizational concept found in hierarchical management structures: the grouping of a single expertise into one specialized silo (department).

Figure B, below, depicts the difference between an Expertise (Silo)-Based Approach and a Function (Value)-Based

Approach. The hierarchical, Expertise (Silo)-Based Approach requires groupings of expertise (e.g., departments) within a company to define their own unique purposes in addition to the overall organization's purpose. To achieve both goals, each department must also create its own unique strategy, enhancements, projects, and maintenance, etc.

In contrast, eco-autonomous organizations propose creating entities containing functions that include multiple capabilities and skillsets spanning a variety of expertise. Each function (strategy, enhancements, projects, and maintenance, for example) includes all of the skills and expertise that function needs to achieve its purpose.

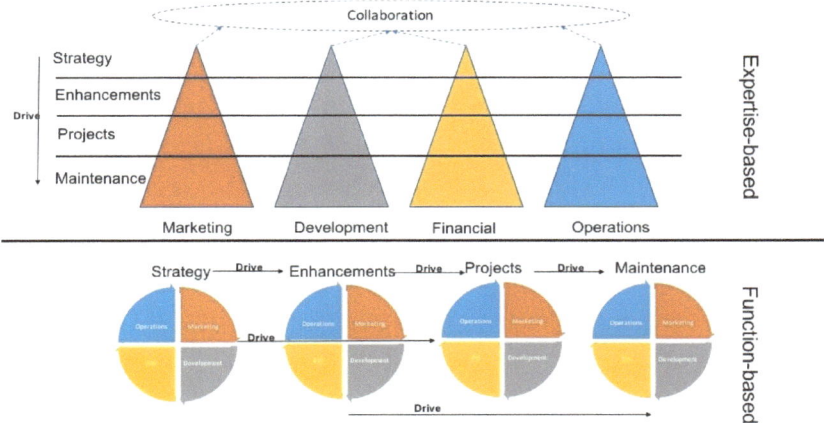

Figure B: Expertise (Silo)-Based Approach vs. Function (Value)-Based Approach

Definitions of Terms

Below is a list of the terms and definitions that will be used throughout this document:

- **Agents:** Agents are groups of individuals, properties and capabilities that interact with other agents to create complex systems. In the business world, agents can be human or mechanical (robots), they may participate in many functions (equivalent to jobs found in hierarchical organizations), and may also be members of several different entities.

- **Function**: A function is a set of rules or models that an agent will follow in response to either 1) feedback received from other agents or 2) an event that occurs within the environment. All functions are unique and should exhibit the following characteristics:
    - A clear purpose that derives from the purpose of the overall entity.
    - A list of responsibilities that define the function.
    - A list of events that trigger the function to react.
    - A set of rules or models that the function will follow in response to an event.
    - A list of relationships to other functions that must exist in order for an agent to perform its particular function.

- A list of artifacts owned by each particular function.

  In the business environment, a function could be series of tasks performed by humans or robots.

- **Externals:** Externals are groups that exist outside of an organization. Examples include customers, stakeholders, competitors and suppliers; financial and research institutions; and even society as a whole.

- **Entities:** Entities are groups of agents, functions and other entities that have a defined purpose and a clear understanding of the value that the entity provides. **Note:** This paper defines five types of entities: systems, ecosystems, planets, solar systems and galaxies. These entity types are recommendations only and can be redefined.

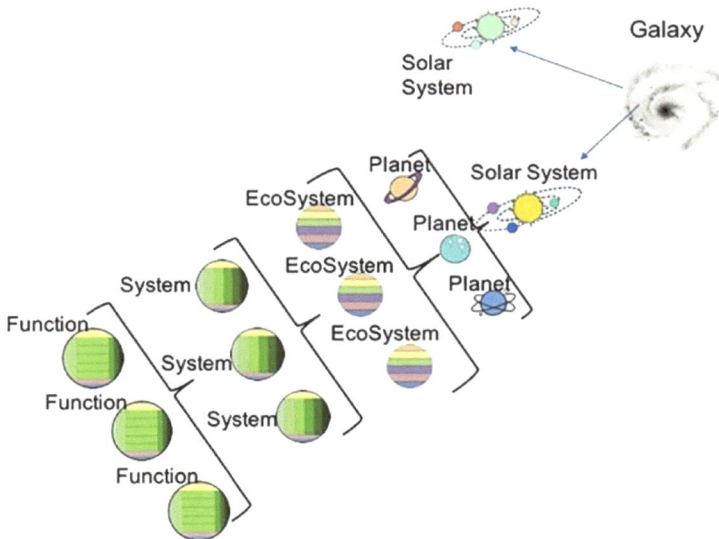

Figure C: Types of Entities

- **System:** A system is a collection of different functions and agents that work together to provide certain defined values (e.g., tasks or projects) to other systems or entities. The distinct inputs and outputs that exist within each system define its contributions.

- **Ecosystem:** An ecosystem is a collection of systems working in harmony to maintain their existence. Ecosystems continually adapt to the environment and may combine with other systems to create part of a value chain that extends to externals.

- **Planet:** A planet is a group of ecosystems working together to deliver either 1) several elements within a value chain for one segment of customers or a part of society or 2) a complete value for different individuals or groups (such as other business owners, financial institutions, etc.).

- **Solar System:** A solar system is a group of planets that gravitate together to provide value for one segment of customers or a certain part of society.

- **Galaxy:** A galaxy is a cluster of solar systems that are held together by a noble idea and provide social and economic value to a society.

The graphic next page depicts each of the organizational elements defined above for a fictional company called ZCommunication:

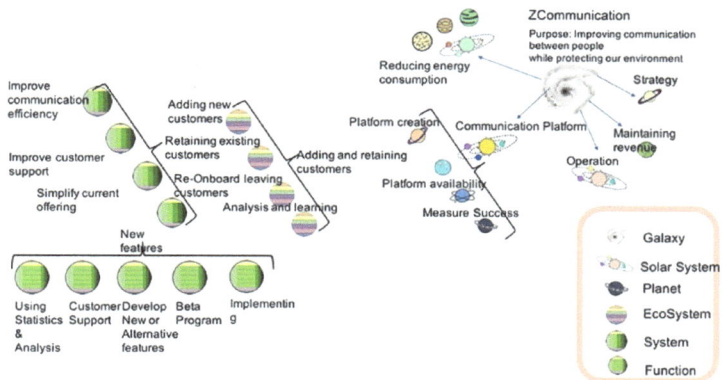

Figure D: Organizational Elements of ZCommunication (a Company)

Agents and Functions

Agents

The people or machines (robots) working within an eco-autonomous organization are agents that perform functions (jobs or tasks) within more than one entity. In alignment with the principles of eco-autonomous organizations and the attributes of complex adaptive systems, this organizational operating structure is designed to break down the silos that exist within many modern organizations.

Agents have the autonomy and authority to make decisions and perform functions at their own discretion. They also have the authority to decide how many hours they need to work, when they want to work those hours, and from what location. In fact, agents have full autonomy over their function as long as all tasks and projects are completed on time and without disruption to other functions or entities. If an agent is unable to complete a task or project as promised, or their actions negatively impact other functions, that agent will be subject to the process defined by the entities he is serving. **Note:** Agent compensation and bonuses are a factor of the number of functions held by an agent and reflect the function's contribution to the overall entity.

While this operating structure is key to creating a viable eco-autonomous organization, agents should be careful not to overcommit to multiple entities when assuming new functions or taking on new tasks. When joining a new entity or starting or performing a new function, being mindful of commitments will help ensure an agent's success within each entity.

Though this method of operation allows organizations to evolve aggressively, it also leaves them vulnerable to human mistakes. To reduce this risk, each agent must design a function to collect data that will allow him, and any other agent, to verify that the evolving function will not introduce a major risk to the system. **Note**: It's each agent's responsibility to verify a function's data against any risks he has encountered.

While autonomy and self-management are key principles of this system, the gap that exists between evolving and chaos also needs to be mitigated. To that end, this chapter defines the behaviors expected from the agents in any galaxy.

Functions

When creating a function, the following questions must be answered:

- What is the purpose of the function?
- What are the responsibilities of the function?
- What are the rules, models and algorithms that the function must follow?
- How does the function connect (internally and externally) with other functions or entities?
- What are the five measurements (or metrics) that will be used to evaluate the function's success?

- What are the artifacts managed by the function?

- Which events will cause the function to react?

- What internal or external feedback loops are in place to monitor the function?

Working with Different Entities

Each of the functions an agent performs and the entities he belongs to may have different rules, policies, principles and procedures, which agents are required to uphold such as attending meetings, providing updates, capturing metrics, or performing any other duties, etc., as defined by each entity. It is the agent's responsibility to be aware of—and follow— these rules, policies, principles and procedures, etc., at all times.

Performing a Function

Self-managing agents are responsible for identifying, logging and prioritizing their projects and tasks. They must also provide project updates to anyone impacted by their work. As part of their function, agents can also initiate new projects and suggest ways to improve the functions they are performing as well as other functions within the entities to which they belong.

While fulfilling a function, agents will receive daily requests from other functions inside and outside of the entity. When an agent receives a request for information or assistance from another agent or function, he must follow these steps:

1. Respond with an assigned priority and estimated delivery timeline (contingent on the level of effort needed and his function's current priorities).

2. Log the request as a project or a task and communicate the delivery date to the requester.

3. Once work begins, an agent must notify the requester immediately if he foresees any obstacles that may cause a deadline to be missed.

4. Upon completion of the task or project, the agent must notify the requester and close the task or project in the log.

If an agent makes a request and receives a reply with an estimated completion deadline that will negatively impact his function:

1. The requesting agent may resubmit the request and ask to renegotiate the delivery timeline, if possible.

2. If renegotiation is not possible, the requesting agent may contact the elected leader (if one exists) of the responding function for assistance. If there is no such leader, the requesting agent may ask the responding agent about his entity's process for resolving conflicts and follow it.

3. To prevent a similar delivery issue from reoccurring in the future, the agent must verify that the request does not require other functions or entities to evolve. (For more information, refer to the **"Evolving" chapter**, page 52.)

While performing functions across multiple entities, agents may witness poor performance by other functions or entities as the result of various events, feedback instances or requests. Upon noticing a poorly performing function, an agent should:

4. Contact the agent responsible for the function and inform him of the issue.

5. If there is no assigned agent or the agent is unavailable, and the witnessing agent has the skillset to resolve the issue, he should:

   1. Step in and resolve the issue.

   2. Contact a related agent, apprise him of the situation, and let him know how it was resolved.

6. If the witnessing agent cannot personally resolve the issue but knows another agent who can, he should:

   1. Contact the agent who can resolve the issue and ask him to resolve it.

   2. Notify the agent responsible for that function, explain what happened, and let him know how the situation was resolved.

7. If the witnessing agent doesn't know anyone who can resolve the problem, he must locate another agent who hosts the problematic function within the entity and inform that agent of the issue.

8. Upon resolution, the witnessing agent must contact anyone who was impacted by the poorly performing function and inform them of its resolution.

Agent Growth and Development

Agents within an organization should take time to work on their own self-awareness, growth and development. Agents that prefer to use goal setting for personal motivation may define a set of annual goals based on their job function, however, goal setting is not mandatory nor is it required.

Any agent who chooses to define a set of goals (or create a personal or professional roadmap) must ensure that those goals/roadmaps support the purpose of 1) the function he is performing, 2) the other entities he supports, and 3) the overall organization. In addition, the agent is solely responsible for following that roadmap and fulfilling those goals.

To begin progress toward self-awareness and development, agents should:

- Identify three areas of improvement quarterly and share them with the team.

- Meet weekly with at least one colleague to seek feedback on the agent's identified areas of improvement.

- Meet weekly with at least one colleague to offer feedback on their identified areas of improvement.

- Provide real-time feedback daily during meetings and other team (or colleague) interactions.

To maintain transparency and work toward continuous improvement, agents should provide their colleagues with daily updates on:

- Tasks completed/accomplishments
- What they've learned (personally/professionally)
- Changes that need to be considered by the Evolving function

Leaving a Function

Agents are invited to apply for functions that match their competencies and skillsets. Once an agent fills a specific function, he is responsible for updating all of the definitions related to that role. As time passes, the duties of that role will continuously evolve by adding and adjusting events, tasks, connections and behavior models. These continual adjustments allow people within an organization to learn, stretch and grow within their roles, eventually leading to new opportunities—or greater responsibilities—within the organization.

At any point, an agent can send a notice to all of the other agents within an entity and inform them that he wants to leave a function within the entity. **Reminder:** Agent compensation and bonuses are a factor of the number of functions held by an agent and reflect the function's contribution to the overall entity.

Agent autonomy and authority go hand-in-hand with accountability; therefore, it is each agent's responsibility to keep his fellow agents informed of any decisions or outcomes that may affect them. When presented with a new function opportunity, each agent has free will and can decide if he wants to accept that opportunity and leave his current function. However, the agent must give appropriate notice to the entity.

Entities

Entities are a collection of functions performed by one or more agents and, like agents, they act autonomously, are self-organized, and self-managed. It's also possible for an entity to be a single function performed by one agent; however, this scenario is atypical.

As part of an entity, agents fulfill a function that supports that entity's purpose or value. The number of functions an agent can fill is unlimited; however, if an entity doesn't have any functions for an agent to perform, then the agent should be removed from the entity.

Following the principle of autonomy, any entity can create and define new entities (or simply ignore those proposed in this paper). In addition, each entity can determine its own unique method for setting internal priorities. This paper recommends that entities base their priorities on both the entity's and its customers' needs. **Note**: Entity priorities will precede function priorities.

Following the attributes of a complex adaptive system, every entity must have a function that is responsible for evolving (i.e., continuously developing into a better entity by identifying ways to improve operations, create new entities, and devise innovative functions). (For more information, refer to the **"Evolving" chapter**, page 52.)

As previously noted, hierarchal relationships do not exist between entities. Therefore, when entities are grouped together for any reason, they need to be given a new grouping name and provided with a reason for the grouping (or purpose) of the entity.

Creating an Entity

If an agent wants to create a new entity, he may take either a "bottom-up" or "top-down" approach. Agents can either start with one entity and one function and then slowly grow their entity (like an embryo) or they can define all five entity types and grow their entities from there. This paper encourages starting with a "bottom-up" approach because any new start may fail and, by starting at the bottom and upward, the impact of failure will be minimized.

When creating a self-organized entity, there aren't any established rules or specific instructions to follow. Each entity creator has the freedom to define how his entity will grow. However, once the entity's agent founder adds other agents, they'll need to work together to set policies, functions and principles, define how the entity will be organized, and outline how its functions will be filled. **Note**: This is a continuous process that can be initiated by any new or existing agent(s).

In addition, each entity must have a clearly defined purpose. In decentralized, autonomous organizations, an entity's purpose is the guiding vision or principle that keeps everyone in the organization reaching for—and working toward—the same goal.

To define an entity's structure, a creator should provide the following information for the entity:

- A clearly defined purpose that is attainable, inspirational, and easy to understand.

- The name of the entity's founder. (This could be an agent's name or the name of a function.)

- The name of the agent filling the pre-defined or custom Evolving function. (For more information, refer to the **"Evolving" chapter,** page 52)

- **Optional:** A definition of the Leader function, plus the name of the elected agent who will fill this function.

- **Optional:** A definition of the alternative Evolving function.

- **Optional**: The Entity Gravity Rules (a list of the rules that keep all functions and agents gravitated together as one entity).

- A list of:

  o All of the principles and policies that all agents within an entity need to follow.

  o All of the entities contained within this entity, including:

    ▪ The entity's connections to (and relationships with) other entities.

    ▪ The definitions for each custom entity (any that are not defined in this paper).

  o The entity's functions, including:

    ▪ All of its agents and their functions.

- The artifacts managed by the entity's functions.

  o The entity's function feedbacks.

  o Metrics (five are recommended to get an accurate picture without consuming too much time) to measure the entity's progress.

  o Unique policies and processes (if defaults are not used), including:

    - Entity communication and conflict resolution processes (how to communicate, sync and resolve conflicts).

    - Separation processes (e.g., how to shut down an entity; how to separate an agent from an entity).

    - Function feedback processes (these should include feedback results in both numeric (metrics) and comment formats).

Filling Functions Within an Entity

Once an entity creator has identified the functions needed to grow an entity, he'll need to add agents to fill those functions. Once these agents have been added, they will be part of the effort to find additional agents to fill new functions. When the new functions are defined, the recommendations provided below (if available) can be used to find the right agent:

- Notify the entity's hiring function.

- Promote the function to all agents within the organization.

- Identify qualified candidates using the galaxy's merit system.

- Interview interested agents.

- Use the entity's merit voting process to determine who will fill certain functions.

It's recommended that each entity establish rules that will help agents gravitate together as one entity (this guidance is especially important for entities containing other entities). These rules should include a collection of behaviors, actions, and checks (algorithms) that agents can follow to determine if they are too far from —or too close to—another entity's agents (or other entities) and what to do in either case. Maintaining appropriate proximity at all times will help autonomous groups remain strong and intact during fluctuations in entities' environments.

Adhering to Entities' Policies and Procedures

When an agent is selected to fill a function within an entity, it's the agent's responsibility to read and understand all of the policies and procedures defined by that entity. When an agent agrees to fill a function, he is also agreeing to follow all of the rules and definitions of the entity.

Agent Autonomy

Every agent filling a function has full autonomy and is authorized to make decisions at his discretion as long as those decisions are in alignment with that function. Each agent should respect the autonomy of other agents. **Note**: Being members of the same entity does not give an agent reason to overrule another agent's autonomy.

Dealing with Dysfunction

An entity may either 1) follow the organization's default policy or 2) establish its own policy for dealing with dysfunctional agents. If an entity determines that an agent is dysfunctional, that entity has the authority to remove the agent from all of the functions he is filling within the entity using a gradual or one-step process. Note: These policies should include opportunities that will allow dysfunctional agents to identify and resolve the root cause of their dysfunction.

Communicating Within an Entity

Each entity must also have a policy that defines how the agents in each function should communicate with each other and keep each other apprised of actions taken on a daily basis. Such policies are put in place to provide effective and efficient methods of communication and to minimize the need for conflict resolution. Any agent filling a function within an entity should be aware of—and follow—that entity's communication policy. This paper proposes that entities use the following default policy:

- Using the entity's chosen communication channel or tool, agents filling at least one function within an entity should:

  - Post a daily update listing the tasks completed, decisions made, roadblocks encountered, risks identified, and mitigations proposed.

  - Read all updates posted daily.

- Agents who feel that a decision or action has impacted (or could impact) a function they're performing should communicate directly with the agent responsible. Agents should also try to resolve any misunderstandings or conflicts directly with the agent(s) involved before requesting support from other entity agents. If the agents are unable to reach an understanding, then the entity's conflict resolution process should be used. **Note**: Involving agents who are not responsible for (or affected by) an impact will create unnecessary clutter.

Scheduling Meetings

Any agent filling a function within an entity has the authority to schedule a meeting and invite all other entity agents to attend if he feels that meeting is necessary. Agents are encouraged to meet on- or offline using any technology they wish for real-time communication. When scheduling a virtual or physical meeting, agents should:

- Send an invitation at least 48 hours before the meeting will occur.

- Include an agenda as well as any relevant reading material with all meeting requests.

- o   Agenda items should be related to entity or function operations and may include requests to:
    - Discuss entity or function metrics.
    - Discuss entity feedback.
    - Change a decision (or decisions) made by another agent due to negative impacts on another entity or function.
    - Discuss the negative impacts an agent's priorities may have on another agent, entity or function.
    - Discuss notes received by other entities.

All meetings should follow the posted agenda. For each agenda item, the requester should:

- Provide at least 15 minutes for all participants to read the submitted materials.

- Give participants time to ask questions related to the submitted materials.

- Present any decisions related to the agenda. **Note**: These decisions should not include changing the definition of an entity or function. These types of changes are part of the evolving process and should be handled during Evolving meetings only.

- If everyone agrees to the proposed decision, then the agent may move forward to the next agenda item. If not, participants must follow the conflict resolution process.

Meetings and sync sessions should include all of the agents within an entity (or all of the agents across all of the entities contained within an entity), as appropriate. However, the idea of "representing" an entity while attending another entity's meeting goes against the concepts of self-management and autonomy; therefore, all agents within a hosted entity should attend the meetings of their contained entities. An exception to this practice may occur if the number of agents in a given entity (including those within its contained entities) exceeds 100 people. In this case, each entity within the containing entity should elect one representative to attend the meeting. Those representatives will then represent the entity and, if merit voting is needed, will submit their votes to represent the merit of all agents represented. **Note**: Because entities do not follow a hierarchy, each representative will only represent the entity to which he belongs (he will not represent any containing entities).

Entity Goal Setting

Entity agents can suggest setting up common yearly goals for an entity. These goals can be set as part of the entity's operational meeting. Once the agents have agreed on the entity's annual goals (with or without the conflict resolution process), the goals will go into effect for all entity agents. These yearly goals are a tool that entities can use to help agents determine the entity's purpose; however, annual goals will not be used to motivate or measure agents' contributions to the entity.

Determining Entity Success and Viability

To continue running, an entity needs to be "alive" and functioning with activities. To monitor these activities and the functions operating them, each entity should have its own metrics and function feedback processes, which are used to determine if (and when) an entity has fulfilled its defined purpose. In general, metric and feedback targets should be set at 100 percent.

If an entity's activities are discontinued and remain inactive for thirty days, a note will be sent to all of that entity's agents. If inactivity continues for 30 more days, the entity should be shut down and moved into "History" mode, where it will remain inaccessible. Once an entity is moved into "History" mode, notification should be sent to all agents. Any agents filling functions within a shutdown entity will be dismissed from that entity's functions. **Note**: When an entity containing other entities is shut down, the shutdown will not impact any contained entities. The contained entities will continue to function as long as they remain alive.

The percentage of entity evolvement (change to adjust to the environment) should also be measured, and entity agents should be notified if evolvement does not occur consistently for at least four months. Lack of evolvement indicates that an entity is in a state of equilibrium, which is not a good sign. Therefore, if evolvement still is not detected after two more months have passed (six months total), then the entity should be shut down and moved to "History" mode.

Dedicated Galaxy Functions

Dedicated galaxy functions collect metrics and feedback for all of the entities contained within a particular galaxy. These dedicated functions will warn all entity (and connected entity) agents in a galaxy when:

- Progress has not been made metrically for three months.

- Negative progress has been made metrically and/or negative feedback has been received during a three month period.

- An entity has received malfunction notes from its own consuming services.

If, after receiving a negative progress warning, progress continues to decline (or another malfunction note is received) over the next two months, the dedicated galaxy function will:

1. Notify all agents and related entities.

2. Shut down the entity and put it into "History" mode.

After these steps are taken, the entity will cease to exist. **Note**: An entity always has the option to shut itself down; however, it *cannot* shut down other entities,

Following an Entity Shutdown

If an entity's functions are still needed following a shutdown, one or both of the following actions may be taken:

- The entity's functions may be added to any other entity that is using the hosting entity's evolving functions. The hosted function can then nominate agents to fill those functions.

- The decommissioned entity can be recreated.

    o In this case, a temporary founder should be assigned by the containing entity. This founder will dedicate the next two months to recreating the entity.

    o Functions within the recreated entity may be filled with agents who are new to the entity entirely or by agents who formerly performed the decommissioned entity.

    o If one or more functions within the recreated entity have not been assigned to or filled by agents, then all of the agents within the containing entity should be responsible for filling those functions. An entity can:

        ▪ Follow standard or customized policies to fill these functions OR

        ▪ Remove these functions from the decommissioned entity and use the Evolving function to transfer them to another entity.

While entities can consume the services or functions of other entities, only the relationships between the entities' functions should be captured within a hosting entity. If an entity determines that a consumed service will better serve the function internally, that entity can define a new function (or functions) and find agents to fill them. Under these circumstances, the same function will be performed by more than one entity. Information gathered through the entity's function feedback mechanism, as well as the functions' own viabilities, will determine which functions will remain over time. **Note**: A shutdown does not need to occur for a function to be operated by two or more entities.

If conflicts arise during recovery of a shutdown entity, agents should follow the organization's default conflict resolution process or the entity's own unique resolution process (if one exists).

The Leader Function

Each entity has the option to establish its own Leader function, which, by default, should be defined as follows:

- **Purpose**: To remove roadblocks, set priorities and resolve daily conflicts.
- **Responsibilities**:
  - Set entity priorities.
  - Assign tasks and projects to functions.
  - Track and analyze entity metrics.
  - Alert entity agents to changes in metrics, as appropriate.
  - Help agents resolve conflicts related to priorities, notes and feedback as they arise.
  - Help agents resolve issues with other entities.

The following steps are needed to create a Leader function:

- The proposed function should have a clearly defined purpose and list of artifacts (tangible assets any function manages).

- The proposed function should be elected at the next scheduled Evolving meeting.

- Any agent within the entity has the authority to propose a candidate to fill this function. The candidate can be anyone inside or outside of the entity, including the nominating agent himself.

- The Leader function will be decided by a regular vote (without merit factor) with the agent earning the most votes winning the role. In the event of a tie, agents will recast their ballots until an agent receives a majority of the votes.

  o For entities that have two agents, the same rules will apply. To fill the Leader function, candidates must receive the support of two agents.

- All entity agents must support the Leader function (not the agent) at all times. If at any time an agent wants to remove support for the Leader function, he can notify all other agents and the function will cease and be removed.

- If an entity is unable to elect an agent to fill the Leader function role, the function will be shared between all of the agents within the entity.

- Prior to the next scheduled Evolving meeting, any agent within the entity can request that a Leader function election occur during the next meeting.

Any agent filling a Leader function role is expected to adhere to the following rules and algorithms. Leader function agents should:

- o Understand the entity's Evolving function and conflict resolution processes and agree to never perform these functions while in the Leader function role.

- o Understand the entity's purpose and priorities before setting any function's priorities. Entity priorities supersede the priorities of any function; therefore, a risk assessment should be conducted on any priorities that could be negatively impacted by the setting of new priorities.

- o Ensure that each task or project assigned to a function supports the entity's overall purpose, projects and tasks.

- o Evaluate the current load of each function before assigning a new task or project to that function.

- o Take responsibility for any conflicts that arise and resolve them.

- o Ensure that assistance provided by the Leader function does not override or interfere with the conflict resolution functions of other entities.

- o Make certain that any requests for help or conflict resolution with other entities does not interfere with the principles of an eco-autonomous organization or the attributes of a complex adaptive system.

Agents in a Leader function should outline processes or procedures for the following:

- Connections with other functions or entities (internal and external), including:

  - All functions within the entity (or other entities grouped together)

  - Any agent fulfilling the leader function

- Measurements or metrics (no more or less than five) used to evaluate a function's success, including:

  - Entity metrics

- Artifacts managed by the Leader function, including:

  - Entity metrics

  - Entity feedback

- Events that the Leader function should react to, including:

  - Any change in entity metrics (positive or negative)

  - New feedback (positive or negative)

  - Requests to resolve conflict

    - If the conflict has been defined for the function, resolve it. If not, initiate conflict resolution through the appropriate process.

- Feedback loops established to receive internal and external feedback

  - A survey should be sent for each service performed or consumed by other entities or externals.

The Evolving Function

Following the attributes of a complex adaptive system, every entity must have a function that is responsible for evolving (i.e., continuously developing into a better entity by identifying ways to improve operations, create new entities and devise innovative functions).

The process of evolution involves accomplishment and failure, therefore, its effectiveness is key for both entity and organization success. Through failure, an entity will learn what *is* and is not working for the entity and the organization; sometimes these lessons can be devastating. Consequently, every entity should have a dedicated function that is responsible for its continuous evolution.

Note: Any change to an entity's purpose, structure, principles, policies, connections and/or relationships with other entities and artifacts indicates that an entity is evolving. However, based on an entity's particular structure, perceived changes such as setting priorities and requests for work are considered operational and are not part of an entity's evolvement.

Understanding the Evolving Function

The Evolving function, a dedicated utility filled by an elected agent who is responsible for the continuous evolution of a particular entity, is the default mechanism used to resolve any expectation-based conflicts that arise from functions within an entity. For example, if one agent expects another agent to perform certain activities or, conversely, *doesn't* expect another agent to perform certain activities, the first agent should seek resolution through the Evolving function, which clearly defines the responsibilities of functions and entities. **Note**: Most conflicts occurring between agents are based on unclear definitions, which can cause differing expectations for the same function or entity.

Every entity has the freedom to use either the default Evolving function (as defined below) or its own customized version. Regardless of whether the function used is default or customized, the Evolving function must follow the core principles of an eco-autonomous organization and the attributes of a complex adaptive system as defined in this paper. However, each entity is also capable of redefining its Evolving function. Therefore, if an entity elects to change the setting of the default Evolving function, then the new function should be redefined for that entity.

By default, the Evolving function should be defined as follows:

- **Purpose**: To continuously evolve and improve an entity.

- **Responsibilities**:
  - Continuously identify and implement better ways to design and operate an entity.

- o Change the purpose of an entity.
- o Add or remove functions and entities.
  - When adding or removing an entity or function, the agent filling the Evolving function should be responsible for making sure the following activities will take place continuously:
    - ❖ keep entity functions and contained entities current with the entity environment
    - ❖ Add, change and/or remove policies, principles, artifacts, connections and/or relationships with other entities.
    - ❖ Elect an agent to fill the Leader function.
    - ❖ Elect an agent to fill the Evolving function.

Following the rules of autonomy, each entity is responsible for its own evolvement. However, the Evolving function only has the ability to change one entity; it cannot change the entities contained within the entity. Although inactivity or dysfunction can shut an entity down (as explained earlier in the **Entities chapter**, page 36), a grouped entity cannot remove the entities contained within it once they are grouped together. However, as also noted in the Entities chapter, the same functions can be recreated and hosted within a different entity. In some instances, duplicated functions may cause the former entity to become dysfunctional or inactive. An exception to this scenario may occur when an entity elects to remove itself following its evolving process.

Electing an Agent for the Evolving Function

There are three events that can trigger the election of an agent to fill the Evolving function. Any of these triggers may begin the Evolving function election process.

1. A new group has been created, which requires an agent to fill the function.

2. The agent currently filling the function wants to be removed.

3. Another agent in the group has requested an election to fill the function.

Elections held to fill the Evolving function will occur during an Evolving meeting. If an elected agent currently runs the Evolving meeting process, that agent will also run the election process. If there isn't an elected agent (or a request for election has been submitted by any agent to reelect existing agent filling the function), then the founder of the entity will run the meeting. If the founder is a robot or is not part of the group, the agent filling the group entity's Evolving function will run the meeting.

The election of an Evolving function agent should be communicated to all entity agents at least 72 hours before the Evolving meeting is scheduled to occur. The meeting notice should include an agenda item that clearly states the reason for—and trigger of—the election.

The Election Process

If there are several items on the meeting agenda, the election will take precedence and occur at the start of the meeting. The election process will proceed as follows.

1. The agent running the meeting will:

    a. Start the process by making a request for nominations. All agents filling functions within the group are eligible for nomination. Agents may also nominate themselves.

    b. Start the election by announcing the names of the agents nominated to fill the function.

    c. Inform all participants that they must cast their votes within the timeframe specified. All agents filling at least one function within the entity are eligible to vote for one candidate. Once the voting timeframe has expired, the agent running the meeting will announce that the voting period has closed.

    d. Tally the votes and take one of the following actions based on election results:

        i. Announce as the elected agent any nominated agent receiving the majority of votes.

        ii. In the event of a tie, the agent running the meeting will immediately hold a second election to break the tie.

            1. If after the second election a tie still exists, the agent running the meeting shall cast his vote to

break the tie and close the election.

   iii. If the elected agent declines to fill the function, the agent running the meeting will remove the elected agent from nomination and immediately hold another election to fill the role.

Evolving Function Rules

Any agent filling an Evolving function should adhere to the following rules and algorithms. Evolving function agents should:

- Follow this guide and alert the appropriate parties if the entity or a function is not following the guide.

- Verify that all requests submitted for the Evolving process occur within the defined process.

- Provide at least 72 hours' notice to all agents within the affected entity before scheduling an Evolving meeting.

- Verify that all meeting requests are scheduled in alignment with the core principles of an eco-autonomous organization and the attributes of a complex adaptive system. If a request is not in alignment with these principles and attributes, the agent should tag the request as "invalid" and explain to the requester why the request has been denied.

- Validate that all requests are new structure changes, policies, principles, connections and/or artifacts. **Note**: Previously rejected requests should not be tagged as "invalid" as a result of this validation.

- Validate that a request to change an artifact won't result in the same artifact being managed by more than one function.

- Validate that any changed function responsibilities won't result in the same responsibility being assigned to two or more functions (in the same entity).

Evolving function connection

- All functions in the entity or other entities that are part of the entity.

- All agents filling any of the functions mentioned above.

Measurements or metrics
- Entity Metrics

Artifacts
- None.

Monitor and act on events that the function should react to:
- Requests to change the purpose of an entity or function.

- Requests to add, remove or change a function, function responsibility, entity, policy, principle, relationship and/or connection.

- Requests for a Leader function election.

- Requests for an Evolving function election.

Feedback loops in place to get internal/external feedbacks

- None.

Handling Requests for Change During an Evolving Meeting

Prior to Evolving meeting, requests not related to an election or the election process should be made in accordance with the default Evolving process:

- Any request for change that is not initiated by the Evolving function should be sent to the Evolving function.

- The Evolving function is responsible for collecting or requesting any data needed to present a change to an entity.

- The Evolving function has the authority to invite externals who are also Subject Matter Experts (SMEs) to discuss the proposed change item with the entity's agents. The number of external SME invited should not be more than 10 percent of an entity's agents. Invited SMEs will participate fully in the entity's Evolving meeting and conflict resolution process.

- Before a proposed change can be discussed, the Evolving function must identify the expertise and competencies required through the Entity Merit Database.

- At least 72 hours before the meeting is held, a meeting request including details on the request for change, the names of the invited external SMEs, agenda items and any supporting data, expertise and competencies should be provided.

- The meeting should focus on the outlined agenda items. Any new requests for change raised during the meeting should be captured but not discussed (unless all meeting participants agree to discuss the new requests at that time).

The Evolving function will decide the order in which the agenda items will be presented and allow time for all participants to read related materials. For each agenda item, the following process should be followed:

- The requester (the agent requesting the change) should explain the request and describe how it will either 1) resolve an existing concern or 2) improve the entity.

- Each participant (including any invited SME) has the option to ask the requester clarifying questions about the proposed change. The requester may answer but is not required to do so.

- Following the meeting, the requester has the option to either 1) request to proceed with the original request 2) adjust his request, 3) postpone the request to a future meeting or 4) cancel the request entirely.

- If the requester wishes to proceed, the request will be put to a vote. All meeting participants should cast one vote for either "Yes," "No," or "Neutral."

- If all meeting participants (which may or may not include all entity agents) vote "Yes" (in favor of) the request, the request should be approved and will go into effect immediately.

- If at least one participant votes "No" (opposes) the request, the Evolving function agent should follow the conflict resolution process for the entity (as defined in the **Resolving Conflict Within an Eco-Autonomous Organization chapter**, page 62).

  - Any decisions made as a result of the conflict resolution process will go into effect immediately. Conflict resolution process results must be respected once they go into effect, however, if an agent later gathers additional data to support a new request for change, that agent may submit a new change request to the Evolving function. Similarly, a request for change can be altered at any time by the submission of a new request by any agent.

- Once the above process has been completed, the Evolving function agent may move to the next item on the agenda. If the time allotted for the meeting runs out and any agenda items remain, discussion of those items should be postponed and added to the agenda for the next meeting.

Resolving Conflict Within an Eco-Autonomous Organization

In an eco-autonomous organization, conflicts exist when at least two agents disagree and the agents involved are unable to reach a resolution that satisfies both parties. Disagreements can arise when:

- A request has been submitted by any agent.

- A decision has been made by any agent.

- An action has been taken by one or more agents.

This chapter describes the default conflict resolution process typically used by an entity, however, each entity has the autonomy to create its own customized process using the Evolving function.

Definitions of Terms

Below is a list of the terms and definitions associated with the default Conflict Resolution Process:

- **Conflict Resolution Coordinator**: This function is typically defined at the galaxy level and can be found within different entities. The agent filling this function is responsible for preparing conflicts for resolution in alignment with the policies and models defined by the galaxy.

- **Change**: A change can be a request submitted, a decision made or an action taken by any agent. **Note**: In this chapter, the word "change" will be used to mean a specific request, decision or action.

- **Requester**: A requester is an agent who initiates any change by:
    - o Take any action or decision to perform his responsibilities.
    - o Ask to change a priority, a task, a project, a function, a policy and/or the definition of a function or entity.

- **Dispute**: A dispute is a disagreement expressed by an agent in response to a change initiated by a requester.

- **Conflicts**: Conflicts are a collection of disputes raised by one or more agents in response to a change initiated by a requester.

- **Disputer**: A disputer is an agent who expresses disagreement with a change initiated by a requester.

The Conflict Resolution Process

The conflict resolution process can be triggered by the Evolving function and can be activated at any time by at least two agents experiencing a conflict based on the function they are performing. When a conflict occurs, one of the following initial actions should be taken:

- If the conflict is first initiated during an Evolving meeting, all of the data needed to discuss the conflict should be made available prior to beginning the resolution process.

- If the conflict is not first initiated during an Evolving meeting, a request for resolution should be sent to the galaxy's Conflict Resolution Coordinator (as detailed in the next section).

Note: Any agent who receives a conflict resolution request must set up a virtual or face-to-face resolution meeting within 48 hours of receiving the request (in alignment with the entity's meeting scheduling process).

Once a conflict resolution request has been initiated, the conflict resolution process should proceed as follows:

1. A request for pre-resolution preparation should be submitted to the Conflict Resolution Coordinator. **Note**: If the coordinator function is also part of the conflict, then the request should be sent to another galaxy coordinator or entity agent whose function is not involved in the conflict.

2. During a conflict resolution meeting, an agent should be elected to run the conflict resolution process. **Note**: Regular election process should be used.

   a. This elected agent should work within the entity (or entities) where the conflict occurred, however, he must not be part of the conflict itself.

   b. If all entity agents are involved in the conflict (e.g., if the change proposed will impact all agents), an assigned external SME should run the process.

3. Once elected, the Conflict Resolution Process Agent or assigned SME has full authority to run the resolution process from this point and make decisions as part of the resolution process.

The Conflict Resolution Coordinator's Role in the Pre-Resolution Preparation Process

Prior to the meeting, the Conflict Resolution Coordinator (or any agent filling that function in the event that the coordinator is involved in the conflict) should follow these steps to prepare for the resolution process. **Note**: These steps are not needed if the resolution process is introduced during an Evolving meeting.

1. Capture and describe in detail the change that is causing the conflict.

2. Capture all of the disputes associated with the conflict.

3. Capture all of the functions and entities associated with the conflict.

4. Identify the agents and/or entities required to attend the meeting based on the functions involved and extend an invitation to them at least 72 hours before the meeting is scheduled to occur. **Note**: If the invited entities follow a different meeting policy, the coordinator should decide which policy is most appropriate for the situation and follow it.

5. Validate that at least one agent who is not part of the conflict is in attendance at the meeting. If all of the invited agents are part of the conflict, the coordinator should find an internal or external SME and invite him to attend. This SME should not have any connection to the agents who are part of the dispute. If all entity agents are involved in the conflict (for example, if the change proposed will impact agents' compensation percentages), the coordinator will need to invite an external SME who is not connected to any of the agents. Once an SME is selected, the person's name should be communicated to all agents so that anyone who may have a connection can inform the coordinator. Only an SME without connections will be selected.

The Conflict Resolution Process Agent's Role in the Pre-Resolution Preparation Process

During the meeting, the elected Conflict Resolution Process Agent should follow these steps to prepare for the resolution process:

1. If there is more than one dispute to discuss, the elected Conflict Resolution Process Agent should review the disputes, remove any duplicate requests, and consolidate the remaining disputes into these categories:

    a. **Dropping Disputes**—Disputes in which the request for change is dropped.

    b. **Adjusting Disputes**—Disputes in which the request for change includes an alternative suggestion for change.

    Note: If the owner of a duplicated dispute disagrees with its removal from the conflict, the Conflict Resolution Process Agent should allow the dispute to remain as part of the conflict until the conflict itself has been discussed and resolved.

2. For each dispute listed within a conflict, the Conflict Resolution Process Agent should validate that the disputes do not conflict with the core principles of an eco-autonomous organization or the attributes of a complex adaptive system as defined within this guide.

3. For each dispute listed within a conflict, the Conflict Resolution Process Agent should also identify the expertise and competencies required to resolve each dispute. This prerequisite task is necessary to facilitate the merit voting process if needed (refer to the Merit Voting section, below).

4. If the Conflict Resolution Process Agent labels a dispute "invalid," the agent must explain why; however, his decision cannot be disputed. Invalid disputes will be automatically rejected. If a disputer disagrees with the Conflict Resolution Process Agent's decision, he is free to submit an entirely new dispute.

Managing the Conflict Resolution Process

The elected Conflict Resolution Process Agent will follow these steps during the conflict resolution meeting to ensure that the process runs smoothly and results in resolution of each conflict.

1. At the start of the meeting, the Conflict Resolution Process Agent should allow time for all attendees to read or review all relevant materials prior to starting the discussion.

2. Once the materials have been read, the meeting should proceed by processing Dropping Disputes one at a time as follows:

   a. Beginning with the "Dropping Disputes" category, the Conflict Resolution Process Agent will review each dispute and invite each disputer to explain his concerns and present the reasons he believes that his dispute should be accepted (dropping review).

   b. After presenting a dropping review, the agent running the system should conduct merit voting as defined in section 3.d.

c. If the majority of the votes support a dropping dispute, the requester decision, action, or request is deemed invalid, and the requester is not allowed to move forward with the disputed action or decision.

d. When a dropping dispute is accepted, all adjusting disputes are not relevant anymore and should not be discussed.

3. After processing all "Dropping Disputes," and if none of them are accepted, the meeting should process all "Adjusting Disputes".

   a. The Conflict Resolution Process Agent will review each adjusting dispute and invite each disputer to explain his concerns and present the reasons he believes that his dispute should be accepted.

   b. After the disputer has presented his case, the Conflict Resolution Process Agent will invite the change requester to explain his point of view and either 1) accept the disputer's concerns and adjust his change request/decision, 2) reject the request and explain his reason for doing so or 3) drop the request and cause the dispute to be labeled "invalid."

      i. If the requester decides to adjust his request and the adjustment is accepted by the disputer, the Conflict Resolution Process Agent can move to the next dispute.

ii. If a dispute is categorized as an "Adjusting Dispute," the disputer should suggest an alternative to the proposed change. **Note**: Raising an Adjusting Dispute without proposing an alternative suggestion must result in the dispute being labeled "invalid" and will negate its ability to be discussed and resolved. Once an "Adjusting Dispute" is approved, the disputer's proposed adjustment will supersede—and replace—the original request.

iii. If an agreement to adjust is not reached immediately, the Conflict Resolution Process Agent should allow the agents in attendance to work together with the requester and disputer on an adjustment that works for both of them.

c. If the disputer and requester do not reach an agreement, any agent participating in the meeting will have the opportunity to express his opinion. After each agent at the meeting has expressed his opinion, the Conflict Resolution Process Agent should hold a merit election, if necessary, to resolve any unresolved conflicts.

d. In accordance with the merit voting process, each agent will be asked to cast his vote and the Conflict Resolution Process Agent will factor in merit based on the list of expertise and competencies previously captured by the Conflict

Resolution Coordinator and the current merit ratings calculated for each participant (as detailed in the Merit Voting section below).

e. Once all agents have cast their votes and merit has been factored in, the Conflict Resolution Process Agent will tally the results. If the tally results in a tie, the Conflict Resolution Process Agent alone will decide whether to accept or reject the dispute.

f. After all disputes have been resolved, the Conflict Resolution Process Agent will hold an election on any change adjustments accepted without a merit vote.

   i. If there are no objections, the conflict is considered resolved.

   ii. If at least one agent votes against an adjusted dispute, the Conflict Resolution Process Agent will begin the resolution process again. **Note**: These steps are needed to allow both the requester and the disputer for each conflict to accept and approve all of the changes made during the process; however, these steps will not trump any decisions made as a result of merit voting.

Merit Voting

The merit voting process allows an organization to factor each agent's expertise and competencies into his vote. Feedback, test results, and decision success rate measurements are used to set an agent's merit level. An agent's merit—which represents an average of all the described datasets in certain expertise or competencies—is ranked numerically from 0 to 100.

To ensure an unbiased understanding of each agent's merit, each galaxy should outline its own definitions of expertise, competencies and collected data. Using the relevant competencies and expertise to address the conflict, the Conflict Resolution Process Agent will factor each agent vote by adding each agent's expertise and competencies merit to their vote and calculating the results. **Note**: To resolve several disputes involving the same agents, different sets of expertise and competencies may be set up to address each dispute.

Voting results are calculated by taking the number of voters and adding the weight of their merit level to their vote. For example, under the normal voting process, if four agents vote and half of the agents support the dispute and half of them oppose it, the result is a 50-50 tie. Once merit voting calculations are factored in, however, that same difference between votes could result in a 60-40 split in favor of the supporters.

If merit vote is needed to resolve a conflict, The Conflict Resolution Process Agent will resolve the dispute based on results of the merit vote. **Note**: This agent is the only person qualified to resolve a dispute; no further objections or disputes can be raised once his decision has been made.

Operating Functions

To operate effectively and improve its chances of success, an eco-autonomous organization must implement certain key operating functions, systems, and processes. This chapter details the different functions needed and explains why they are important for the survival of a complex adaptive system.

Effective Communication Tools

To thrive and evolve over time, every living organism must find a way to communicate. Therefore, without effective communication processes, complex adaptive systems and eco-autonomous organizations are likely to fail.

Despite the many methods humans have devised to make communication faster, easier, and more effective, all existing tools have been deemed too distractive for distributed organizations. Therefore, any organization using this paper as its operating system should find or develop better communication tools.

Agent Related Processes and Policies

This section explains the default Agent Related processes and policies that should be implemented within an eco-autonomous organization. Each galaxy has the freedom to use the default process described below or create its own customized process. **Note**: All entities within a given galaxy must follow that galaxy's agent related processes unless stated explicitly in this paper.

The agent related function (or agent related entity) must follow all of the core principles and attributes of a complex adaptive system while maintaining its focus on multi-functional agents and transparency. This paper advises selecting an agent related SME that is part of the agent related entity to fill the agent related function. This SME shall encourage the agent related entity to be multi-disciplined by recruiting other agents possessing a variety of expertise.

Vacation Policy

As stated previously in the **Agents and Functions chapter** (page 28), each agent has the autonomy to decide the timing and duration of his personal vacation time. There is no imposed limit on the number of vacation days an agent can take, however, each self-managed agent should be aware of the impact that the timing and number of days taken will have on his function and the functions of other agents within the organization. Vacation decisions should be made with these impacts in mind at all times.

To ensure that impact is minimal, each agent should follow the organization's communication process to properly inform other agents of a vacation's timing and duration, allowing impacted agents enough time to raise a conflict if they feel the decision will negatively affect them.

Hiring Process

Each galaxy should have a Hiring entity responsible for adding the right agents to the galaxy. This entity should be tasked with continually identifying any current hiring gaps and taking action to find qualified candidates who can fill those gaps and also perform successfully within a self-managed environment. This process should continue as long as its efforts can be supported financially by a galaxy.

The hiring philosophy of an eco-autonomous organization is different than the approach used by traditional management systems. Eco-autonomous organizations should consistently search for people who can fill existing gaps *and* the future needs of the organization. To ensure that the best and brightest talent is always within reach, the Hiring entity should continually publish a list of functions based on current and future hiring needs. Published functions should clearly define which expertise and competencies are needed to ensure successful performance.

When a Hiring entity receives a candidate's application, the process of validating the candidate's fit with the function will begin. The process should include several methods of validation including tests, human interactions inside and outside of the galaxy, and fit both within the function and also within galaxy culture. Taking into account any cognitive biases, the hiring process should emphasize different tests defined specifically for each function. These tests will be used to verify a lack of bias and ensure that the right people are being selected and hired.

Note: An eco-autonomous organization's practice of hiring according to function allows applicants to choose the amount of time they want to spend within a particular galaxy. Each agent has the freedom to fill or leave a function at any time. However, as mentioned in the **Agents and Functions chapter** (page 28), deciding to leave or fill a function will have an impact on an agent's earnings.

New Hire Onboarding

Any agent joining an eco-autonomous organization for the first time should go through an onboarding process that will acclimate, train and slowly acquaint them with their new work environment and its unique methods of operation.

Each galaxy (and its entities) should have at least one Onboarding function responsible for the onboarding of new agents. The entity housing that function shall have the freedom to follow the default process described in this chapter or create its own customized version. This paper suggests that the Onboarding function be performed as described; however, each entity has the autonomy to define how its functions will be performed.

The purpose of the Onboarding function is to ensure that all new agents have the knowledge, experience and tools needed to successfully perform their roles and acclimate to the galaxy's culture. The Onboarding function should ensure that each new agent has:

- The equipment needed to successfully fulfill his function(s).

- The accessibility rights needed for any systems critical to the operation of his function(s).

- Access to an onboarding buddy who will help the new agent acclimate to organization culture during his first two months of work.

- Access to a technical coach (if needed) who will guide him through the technical aspects of his function(s).

- Access to the agent with the highest merit in the core principles of an eco-autonomous organization, who will be available to explain these principles and why it is important to follow them.

- Access to the agent with the highest merit in the attributes of a complex adaptive system, who will be available to explain these attributes and why they are important.

- Knowledge of any custom requirements that must be set up by the entities the new agent is joining.

- Knowledge and understanding of the Evolving function.

- Knowledge and understanding of the conflict resolution process.

The two-month onboarding period is an opportunity for new agents and their entities to ensure there is a successful cultural fit. After joining, if at any point a new agent feels like the culture is not the right fit for him, he can inform the galaxy's agent related function and begin the separation process.

Once the onboarding process has ended, the agent related function should reach out to each new agent and their onboarding buddy to collect feedback. A feedback value between 1 and10 should be assigned for each feedback topic:

- Fit to work in the environment.

- Fit to fulfill assigned functions.

- Competencies and expertise related to functions being filled.

An agent's feedback value results and the decisions made based on those results (i.e., to begin the separation process or not) should be communicated to all agents who were part of the feedback collection process. If any agent has a conflict with the decision being made, that agent may initiate a conflict using the entity's conflict resolution process.

Compensation Policy Model

The compensation policy model for any galaxy should follow the core principles of an eco-autonomous organization and the attributes of a complex adaptive system with a focus on transparency. As always, each galaxy has the ability to set its own customized compensation model or use a default model. Under either model version, each galaxy is a unique profit center and should have its own method for generating revenue. Some galaxies may generate revenue by charging other galaxies for their services. **Note**: Galaxies set up for social good are the only exception to this rule.

This paper suggests that each galaxy allocate a percentage of its revenues to all entities defined within that galaxy, based on each entity's individual contributions to the galaxy. Each entity within a galaxy can distribute its percentage between their contained entities and functions. When a new entity (or function within an entity) is added or removed, the compensation percentage that exists between all of the entities (or functions) supporting the contained entity should be reallocated. This recursive allocation should run until all functions receive a percentage in compensation.

Agent compensation should be based on the functions being filled based on the percentage allocated to each function he is filling. Although an agent may join one galaxy, it's possible they might also be engaged with—and fill functions within—other galaxies. If this is the case, an agent's total compensation will be the sum of his compensation within all of the galaxies for which he performs functions. **Note**: This proposed compensation model is based on agents' contributions to entity and galaxy success, not on the number of hours an agent works each month. This model enables any individual to fill any function (or functions) based on the amount of effort and length of time he chooses to spend within an organization.

Some functions in any entity might have zero percentage allocated to them. One example is training function created to support Agent growth. One way or another the Entity is the only one who should decide how allocated percentage will be separate between all functions and contained entities.

The compensation percentage allocated to each function should be available at any time to all galaxy agents. Based on the function being filled, each agent should have full transparency into the compensation received by other agents. If any agent within that entity objects to his level of compensation, he can initiate a conflict using that entity's conflict resolution process.

This compensation model doesn't have a minimum or maximum amount allotted to it. Each agent's compensation is based on his contribution to the entity and the collective profit that all of the entities within a galaxy earn each month. If a galaxy allocates a certain percentage of its revenue toward bonuses, the bonus percentage (based on the galaxy's financial results) will be split equally between all agents filling a function within that galaxy.

Career Advancement and Promotions

Based on the compensation model described above, the default agent related function does not contain a process for career advancement or promotions. In a hierarchical management system, promotions are designed to help people move up the leadership chain—and increase their compensation—as their "contributions" to the company expand. However, the operation model of an eco-autonomous system is not based on hierarchy and its compensation model does not include minimum or maximum guidelines. Instead, this system is based solely on each individual's contribution to the galaxy and its profits.

Personal and Professional Development

The practice of continuous personal and professional development is a key activity that strongly aligns with the core principles of an eco-autonomous organization and the attributes of a complex adaptive system. Therefore, each galaxy should have at least one function that is responsible for personal and professional development.

Professionally, agents should strive to continuously improve the expertise required to perform one or more functions. They can also create a new expertise to expand the breadth of their knowledge. Regardless of the topic they choose to explore (accounting, jewelry design, painting or programming for example), the journey toward improvement should be ongoing.

Agents are also encouraged to grow personally by developing a deeper understanding of 1) the cognitive biases that drive their own and others' behavior; 2) the kind of activities or behavior that motivates them and those around them; and 3) the types of behavior that may be perceived as risky or unacceptable. This personal development journey should focus on strengthening agents' competencies and building their potential as human beings.

Note: Personal development assessments *should not* be used for any purpose other than personal development. However, if an agent's consent is provided, his assessment can be shared with other agents and/or external service providers.

Development Training

Any agent filling at least one function in a galaxy has the autonomy to decide what type of training he needs to further his development. This decision does not require approval— agents are free to participate in any training course or program they choose. However, agents must ensure that their functions and entities will not be negatively impacted by their decision to participate in training and are required to inform other agents through the entity's communication process. If any agent disagrees with the timing of a training (or any other impact), he is free to raise a conflict in accordance with the conflict resolution process.

Training is considered an expense and any agent who chooses to attend a training course, program, event or festival for self-awareness will need to fill out an expense report and submit it in accordance with the entity's expense report process (refer to the Budget and **Financial Control Processes section**, page 90).

The Continuous Feedback Process

Transparent, near real-time (or continuous) feedback is essential for all development. When provided consistently and in a timely manner, feedback helps agents understand the context of their coworkers' reactions and provides an opportunity to address any concerns that may arise before they turn into conflicts. To ensure that feedback is effective, it should be provided:

- As close as possible to the event, behavior or action that has occurred.

- Directly to the agent receiving the feedback by the person delivering the feedback. If this is not possible, the name of the person providing the feedback should be shared with the receiver.

Measuring Merit

Businesses that have leveraged meritocracy successfully have done so by using data, facts and results to calculate merit. Before implementing a merit measuring process, ensure that each agent understands that merit will be calculated using data and an agent's history of successful decisions only—cognitive bias and emotions will not be a factor.

This paper suggests calculating an agent's merit based on:

- Unbiased and neutral assessments of an agent's competencies and expertise.
- An agent's record of decisions, which have been tracked and tagged as "successes" or "failures" based on facts (data).
- Feedback provided by other agents.

As mentioned previously in the **Resolving Conflict Within an Eco-Autonomous Organization chapter** (page 62), each galaxy should define and maintain a list of the competencies and expertise needed to fill its functions and act in accordance with these guidelines:

- At least once every two years, a galaxy's list of competencies and expertise should be evaluated.
- The addition or removal of competencies should involve an external SME due to a need of knowledge and experience in psychology.
- The addition or removal of competencies or expertise should be communicated to all galaxy agents.
- The addition or removal of competencies or expertise shall be subject to conflicts raised by any agent within the galaxy.

If any agent has a dispute with the calculated merit, that agent should use the conflict resolution process to raise the dispute.

Before the Conflict Resolution Coordinator schedules a meeting, however, the dispute should be sent to the Merit entity for validation of the merit calculation. **Note**: The results of the conflict resolution process will trump the merit calculation and, if the conflict resolution process changes the way that merit is calculated, that change will apply to all agents.

The Separation Process

Over the course of an agent's career, it's possible that an agent could lose one or more functions within an entity under the following circumstances:

- A function or entity has been switched into "History" mode due to poor performance.

- An entity has been switched into "History" mode due to lack of evolvement.

- A function or entity has been switched into "History" mode due to inactivity.

If, for any of the reasons above, an agent is left without one or more functions to fill, he will automatically be granted two weeks to find a new function. During that time, the agent will receive payment equal to the average compensation earned from all of the functions he performed prior to being without one or more functions. However, if during that time period the agent is unable to find a new function to fill, the agent related entity should start the separation process. **Note**: Any agent who has lost all of his functions has the freedom to apply to fill any functions that are posted in the future.

Any violation of ethics; an organization's core principles; and/or the attributes of a complex adaptive system should be raised to the galaxy agent related function for evaluation. Upon confirmation, the agent related function can and must follow the separation process.

Budget and Financial Control Processes

Each galaxy, as an independent cost center, should have an entity responsible for creating and managing a budget and providing financial control services to the galaxy. As always, the Budget and Financial Control entities must follow the core principles of an eco-autonomous organization and the attributes of a complex adaptive system.

Budget

This paper suggests that the Budget function or entity will collect budgetary information from all functions within an entity and, based on collected data (such as the entity's prior year's performance, industry forecasts, and current trends in the global economy), will adjust the final budget to fit the entity's needs. All details should be transparent and available to any agent filling any function in the galaxy's entities.

If a galaxy experiences a radical change that requires a major cost reduction, a decision to reduce the number of agents will not automatically be considered as the default option. Instead, the galaxy will reduce the total compensation amount allocated from revenue generated by the galaxy.

Expense Reporting Process

In alignment with the core principles of an eco-autonomous organization and the attributes of a complex adaptive system, each galaxy has the freedom to define its own Expense function, entity or process (or use a default process) as described below:

- Any payment made on behalf of the organization by an agent while performing a function should be recorded through the filing of an expense report. The report should include:

    o The name of the function for which the goods or services were purchased.

    o A description of the goods or services purchased.

    o The exact amount of money spent.

Expense reports should be sent directly to the Budget entity or function. Expense reports will not be approved or rejected. Instead, a monthly breakdown of all agents' expense requests (including the total amounts requested and the services or goods consumed for each function) should be sent to each agent within the galaxy. Any agent objecting to an expense can raise a dispute using the conflict resolution process. If the expense is deemed "invalid" as a result of the conflict resolution process, the agent who filed the expense report should pay for the disputed expense.

Financial Control

Based on expense reports, invoicing and depreciation, the
Financial Control entity should create a report that shows the
actual spending per entity versus the entity's monthly and
year-to-date budget. The Financial Control entity should
define which percentage of deviation from the budget must
be explained. Based on this definition, each entity above or
below the deviation must provide an explanation to the
Financial Control entity within a week of receiving the report.
The final report, with comments, should be shared with all
galaxy agents.

The Financial Control entity has the right to limit an entity's
spending if it repeatedly exceeds the budget. In this case, the
Financial Control entity should ask the entity to balance its
spending by removing certain budget items from its project
list for the current year.

Prioritization, Planning and Execution

This chapter explains how prioritization, planning and execution should occur within a decentralized and distributed organization where a central decision-making authority does not exist.

Prioritization

Priorities are used in the planning process to help agents know which requests should be focused on first. Therefore, each project, activity or request that an agent needs to perform while filling a function should be assigned a priority and an estimated time of delivery.

As mentioned earlier in the **Agents and Functions chapter** (page 28), each agent has the autonomy to decide which priority a given request will be assigned. If a requester feels that the priority and estimated time of delivery assigned by an agent will negatively impact his function, the requester can raise a dispute using the conflict resolution process.

Note: Priorities associated with just one function or entity should be easy to manage, however, handling requests that come in from several different entities—both internally and externally, and with conflicting priorities—can become more complex to manage over time.

Entities are not arranged hierarchically; therefore, it is common for entities and functions supporting the same purpose to be grouped or contained within more than one entity. Each entity has the autonomy to define its own priorities and, as such, does not need to follow the priorities defined by its hosting entities (unless it chooses to do so). However, there are four ways that a hosting entity can influence the entities that compose it. It can:

1. Convince the contained entities that they should follow certain priorities (as defined by the hosting entity).

2. Request a resolution using the conflict resolution process.

3. Change the entities' compensation percentage to reflect their decreased support of the hosting entity's goal. **Note**: This decision is subject to dispute.

4. Create an internal function within the contained entity that will allow it to follow the hosting entity's priorities. **Note**: Although this option will create the desired solution, it may also create duplication within the entity.

Planning

Any entity (and all agents filling functions within that entity) should follow a short work cycle (two weeks) and use that cycle to estimate how long a request will take to complete. In each cycle, the entity should formulate a plan based on the prioritization of requests received.

To turn each request into a task and plan how many work cycles will be needed, agents can use any tool or method they feel is most convenient. Once a date of delivery is determined, an agent must communicate that date to the requester.

Based on an entity's work cycle, an agent may need to adjust his priorities to accommodate new requests or satisfy a decision made by the Conflict Resolution Process function. If priorities are changed, the agent receiving the request must adjust his work cycles and inform all impacted agents.

Note: To maintain transparency throughout a work cycle, it's important that agents keep all requesters apprised of their initial priority assignments and times of delivery as well as any subsequent updates made.

Execution

While working through a cycle, no new requests should be added to an agent's workload. The only changes that can impact an agent's schedule are issues that arise unexpectedly and require his assistance to keep the default activities of a function or entity running. New requests received during a work cycle will be queued and addressed at the next cycle planning meeting.

An agent should immediately contact the requester and inform him of any issues or challenges that arise while working on a request. If an agent needs feedback from a requester before continuing the next stage of a project, he should share his needs with the requester and ask for feedback. It's better for an agent to receive that feedback and adjust endure a complete rejection of the work upon completion.

Data and Analysis

In an eco-autonomous organization, the compilation and analysis of data are essential for continuous improvement, sound decision-making, progress measurement and transparency. Therefore, organizations should collect as much as data as possible about the activities performed by each agent and/or entity, as well as collecting data on all events, actions and results. If certain data is not needed today, it can be stored for future use.

The Distribution of Classical Managerial Authorities

This chapter is a guide for anyone experienced with classical managerial organization. The outline below explains how classical managerial authorities and responsibilities are handled within eco-autonomous organizations.

- Providing guidance to direct reports.
  - In an eco-autonomous organization, direct reports do not exist. Each agent is expected to manage himself using the organization's core principles, attributes, purpose and metrics as a guide. However, if all entity agents agree, an agent can be elected to fill the Leader function (or design another guiding function) to fill that role. However, the Leader function will not replace an organization's core principles, attributes, purpose or metrics. Together, these elements form the compass that all agents should follow. An agent's personal and professional development (and coaching) should also provide guidance when needed.
- Ensuring clarity around priorities and goals; translating corporate goals into functional and individual goals.
  - Purpose is what driving Agents in EcoAutonomous organizations
  - Goals are not required, however, they can be defined by entities and functions as follows:

- Each entity and function should have a defined purpose that also serves as its goal.

- Each entity may define yearly goals for all of its functions.

- Each may should have its own defined goals.

  - Regarding priorities, each entity and agent should assign priorities to projects and tasks. However, while an entity can't enforce priorities on contained entities, an entity's functions should uphold its entity's priorities.

- Approving investment requests; monitoring and controlling expenses and budgets.

  - Agents have the authority to request funds for investment into new projects or technologies and to ask for reimbursement for expenses related to their functions.

  - Investments and expenses reduced from galaxy revenues will impact all agents' compensation. Although each galaxy should have a dedicated function that is responsible for budget planning and monitoring, any agent can a raise conflict regarding any expense. In accordance with the conflict resolution process, conflicts should be resolved between agents when possible and the resolution process should be used if an agreement cannot be reached.

- Managing budgets.

  - A galaxy's budget is planned and managed by a dedicated function or entity within the galaxy. This function receives requests for new investments from all agents, tracks financial needs, and translates requests into the yearly budget. This process is transparent and subject to dispute by any galaxy agent.

- o The yearly budget is transparent and available for review by any agent at any time. The Budget function agent is responsible for finding monies needed to fund any unplanned projects or events that arise during the year. In addition, this agent must notify and take action against any agents in violation of the yearly budget.

- Managing agent hirings and firings.

- o The hiring process is based on non-subjective evaluations and tests. Each galaxy should have a function or entity responsible for continuously identifying the need to hire new agents and initiating and coordinating the hiring process based on that need.

- o A galaxy's Hiring function or entity can make the decision to hire any new agent.

- o Following the onboarding period, every new agent should be evaluated to assess his ability to fit both within the function and also within the organization's culture. Fit and performance assessments will be provided by all agents interacting with the new hire.

- o The separation process can be initiated by any agent. Depending on the cause, the separation process might involve the galaxy's agent related function.

- o Reasons for initiating the separation process with an agent include violation of ethics; an organization's core principles; and/or the attributes of a complex adaptive system. Separation may also occur if an agent is left without any functions to fill. **Note**: Except in the case of an ethics violation, the separation process is subject to dispute.

- Guiding the talent identification and development processes; coaching and developing existing employees.

  o In self-managed organizations without central authorization and decision-making practices, each agent is responsible for his own personal and professional development. While there are entities and functions available to help with this process (mainly by providing coaches that can help agents with their development and offer advice when difficulties arise), it's each agent's responsibility to seek help and make sure development occurs.

  o An agent's merit in different competencies and expertise can also help determine where talents exist or need growth. This information is available for any agent to view and can also be used by entities that want to hire agents to fill new or empty functions.

- Working across functions with peers in other groups to ensure collaboration on shared goals.

  o Related and connected functions and entities are recorded as part of an entity's definition and are available for any agent to view. By definition, eco-autonomous organizations are built from groups that contain all of the expertise needed to achieve a certain purpose. Agents with certain types of expertise may join different entities and routinely collaborate with agents who possess varying types of expertise. Because each agent is part of a cross-functional entity (or entities), this No-Silo organizational structure does not require managerial roles that work across functions.

- Interacting with (or reporting to) management.

  o In a self-managed organization, the manager-subordinate reporting structure does not exist. Instead, the No-Silo organizational approach creates hybrid teams that force all agents to interact, contribute different types of expertise, and fulfill various functions. Eco-autonomous organizations provide all agents with direct connections to other agents filling similar or related functions. This direct communication channel makes it easier for agents to perform tasks and achieve goals accurately and efficiently.

- Working with senior management and other peers on strategy development, planning and execution.

  o Strategy development, planning and execution functions or entities should be created by galaxies when needed.

  o Each function and entity has the autonomy to set its own execution plan.

  o The Strategy function or entity is typically run by a group of agents with different backgrounds; those agents have the authority to decide how the function or entity will be run.

- Communicate financial results, goal results and key performance indicators to direct reports.

  o Each agent has transparent real-time visibility into entity metrics, which depict how each entity is performing toward its goals.

- Supporting problem resolution and decision-making.

- In an eco-autonomous organization, these practices have been replaced by the conflict resolution process, which uses merit-based voting to resolve conflicts by factoring in: 1) agents' different levels of knowledge and experience; 2) the Conflict Resolution Process Agent's unbiased understanding of the context of a dispute; and 3) other related, past experience.

- Conducting timely performance evaluations and initiating action to strengthen results.

  - Instead of conducting performance evaluations, eco-autonomous organizations address performance by sharing revenue between all agents based on function and initiating the separation process for agents left without functions to fill. Classical feedback processes are replaced by real-time, 365-degree feedback loops provided by the agents, customers and service providers interacting with each agent.

Where to learn more

If you made it to this chapter, you are really keen to learn or implement new ways to operate and structure organizations. We hope that this book helped you to realize a new approach that fits better with today's world and the future. If you have any comments or questions regarding this book, please share it with our community at **www.ongalaxies.com**.

Hierarchical organization comparing to Eco Autonomous Organization

Hierarchical Org Vs EcoAutonomous organization		
	From	**To**
Organization Are: (Philosophy)	Machines	Living Organism
Organization Focus	Efficiency	Disruption
Organize People	Central control	Decentralize
	Management	Self Mgmt. Self Org.
	Steer By Board and Committee	Steer By Environment
	Silos / Expertise	Hybrid Teams
Motivate People	Promotions (fixed income)	% of revenue (based on contribution)
	Appraisals & Reviews	360 (Transparent) Feedback
	Fear	Trust

Notes

i https://www.towerswatson.com/Insights/IC-Types/Survey-Research-Results/2012/07/2012-Towers-Watson-Global-Workforce-Study

iihttps://www.forbes.com/sites/causeintegration/2017/06/01/employee-engagement-is-declining-worldwide/#bb7477634e2f

iii https://www.forbes.com/sites/elainepofeldt/2017/10/17/are-we-ready-for-a-workforce-that-is-50-freelance/#7d211d5b3f82

iv http://www.aei.org/publication/fortune-500-firms-1955-v-2017-only-12-remain-thanks-to-the-creative-destruction-that-fuels-economic-prosperity/

v https://www.inc.com/ilan-mochari/innosight-sp-500-new-companies.html

vi Ronald Nason's "It's Not Complicated: The Art and Science of Complexity for Business Success
https://www.amazon.com/s/ref=dp_byline_sr_ebooks_1?ie=UTF8&text=Richard++Ronald+Nason&search-alias=digital-text&field-author=Richard++Ronald+Nason&sort=relevancerank

vii Schmitt, A., Den Hartog, D. N., & Belschak, F. D. (2016). Transformational leadership and proactive work behaviour: A moderated mediation model including work engagement and job strain. Journal Of Occupational And Organizational Psychology, 89(3), 588-610. doi:10.1111/joop.12143

www.ingramcontent.com/pod-product-compliance
Lightning Source LLC
Chambersburg PA
CBHW041716200326
41519CB00005B/264